684.1009
Cᴏ

T00684

HANDMADE WOODWORK OF THE TWENTIETH CENTURY

The choice lies with each one of us as individuals—
to build up, or destroy. As for the artist and
craftsman, he has no enemy but time; life is all too
short for learning his job and doing it well. He
cannot start too young nor live too long.

JOHN FARLEIGH
The Creative Craftsman

Title pages
Interior of part of Edward
Barnsley's workshop in 1947,
which has since been considerably
enlarged.
Far right: Herbert
Upton, Foreman-
Manager.

Handmade Woodwor

A. E. BRADSHAW

the Twentieth Century

JOHN MURRAY *Fifty Albemarle Street, London*

BY THE SAME AUTHOR

Woodcraft for Schools and Colleges
Reading and Making Technical Drawings

TO

MY WIFE

whose patience and assistance
have made this book possible

© A. E. BRADSHAW 1962
First edition 1962
Second edition 1965
Printed in Great Britain by
Jarrold & Sons Ltd, Norwich

CONTENTS

ACKNOWLEDGMENTS

I regret that it is not possible to mention individually all the people who, over the years, have assisted in the production of this book, so I hope that all who have helped in any way—including those who allowed special photographs to be taken—will accept my thanks.

I acknowledge gratefully my indebtedness to all the modern designer-craftsmen and the colleges who are listed in the Index. My thanks are due in particular to the many friends who have, in one way or another, commented upon the manuscript and especially to Edward Barnsley, Esq., C.B.E., Sir George L. Trevelyan, Bart., M.A., and A. W. Wilkins, Esq., O.B.E.

Any merit that the book may have is consequently due to the co-operation of many people. Its shortcomings are due to my own limitations.

Her Majesty Queen Elizabeth II has graciously permitted the reproduction of the photograph on page 119. Thanks are due also to the following who have kindly allowed copyright photographs to be used:

OWNERS OF COPYRIGHTS
Council of Industrial Design 1, 25 (*bottom*), 72, 110, 112, 113 (*bottom*), 118 (*top*)
Victoria and Albert Museum 2, 3 (*top*)
Messrs. Heal and Son, Ltd 4–6
George Roper, Cirencester 7–16, 22
Messrs. Gordon Russell Ltd 28–31
Rural Industries Bureau 32 (*top*), 73 (*both*)
Stanley W. Davies 38–39
The Hampshire Chronicle 40
Eric Sharpe 41
Wood 53
Ideal Home 70
Messrs. Entwistle, Thorpe & Co. Ltd 76 (*top*)
Cheltenham Art Gallery and Museum 99 (*top*)
The Tate Gallery 99 (*bottom*), 103
Woodworker 88
Associated Press 120
Arthur W. Mitchell, 9 (*top*), 18 (*top*), 19 (*bottom*), 21 (*top*), 23 (*both*), 24 (*both*)
Christopher Smedley 109

INTRODUCTION TO THE SECOND EDITION

The call for a second edition of this book has given the author the opportunity to revise and expand the text and to introduce many more illustrations.

It is an interesting feature of this industrial age, when most of our household goods are of necessity mass-produced, that thero is still a place in our economy for the individual 'designer-craftsman' who makes things by hand in the traditional way. Today there are craftsmen and craftswomen in many 'fine crafts'—potters, weavers, silversmiths and many others, as well as furniture makers—working in small workshops up and down the country, and producing work of high quality and individuality. For each of these fine crafts and its survival in the present day there is a story to be told. The designer-craftsman makers of furniture occupy a small but important place alongside, but largely independent of, the massive furniture industry. What that place is, how the craft has developed during this century, and the substance of the tradition within which the hand craftsman works: these make up the theme of this book.

To understand the craftsman's way of working one must look further back. Let us begin by considering the eighteenth century, when the famous cabinet-makers—Chippendale, Hepplewhite and Sheraton—were designers for the important and fashionable people. We will also find the culmination of the tradition of English country furniture making—the work of humble unknown craftsmen who made the furniture for cottage and farmhouse out of the common English timbers. In the eighteenth century we see the end product of five hundred years of development just before it was overtaken by the rise of industrialization. Today we collect such pieces of work and treasure them and put them into museums and into our homes if we can. From museum collections and from books we can see the development of five centuries: how the craft has grown from crude beginnings, how ideas of construction have evolved and methods improved as tools improved, how furniture developed to meet ever-expanding household needs, and how an unpretentious functional design grew up closely linked with the craftsman's ways of working. This is the true English furniture tradition, and the designer-craftsman of today has a close affinity with it, for his methods are, basically, similar. He may, of course, use power tools for the preparation of his material, and also, if he wishes, for other mechanical and repetitive operations, but for the hand work which follows he uses much the same tools, constructions and methods as were used by craftsmen of earlier days.

This traditional craft, so much a part of English life, was almost swallowed up by the rise of industrialization in the nineteenth century. It may be doubted if the individual craftsman, working in the old ways, was altogether extinguished; but there can be no doubt that the effect of booming industrial production was to threaten his livelihood and to debase his standards, especially of design. If we look at the industrial goods shown in the Great Exhibition of 1851 we can see little place there for the craftsman, or for his notions of how to design and make furniture. The biographer of William Morris, J. W. Mackail, writes that when Morris and his friends began to furnish the Red House at Bexley in 1859, 'Not a chair, or table, or bed; not a cloth or paper hanging from the walls; nor tiles to line fireplaces or passages; nor a curtain or a candlestick; nor a jug to hold wine or a glass to drink it out of, but had to be reinvented, one might almost say, to escape the flat ugliness of the current article.'

There is hardly an important English fine craft which has not been influenced, directly or indirectly, by William Morris, and a number of crafts owe their revival, and indeed their survival, to him alone. The colourful life of Morris has been the subject of many books, and should be familiar to the serious student of any fine craft.

There is hardly an important English fine craft which has not been influenced, directly or indirectly, by William Morris, and a number of crafts owe their revival, and indeed their survival, to him alone. The colourful life of Morris has been the subject of many books, and should be familiar to the serious student of any fine craft. Nikolaus Pevsner gives an architect's view (*Pioneers of Modern Design*, 1949): 'We owe it to him (Morris) that an ordinary man's dwelling house has become once more a worthy object of the architect's thought, and a chair, a wallpaper, or a vase a worthy object of the artist's imagination.' A craftsman would add that we owe it to Morris also that the traditional crafts of this country are still alive in our day, the fine craft of furniture making amongst them. But in this craft the direct influence has come from men who knew Morris and were inspired by him rather than directly from Morris himself. It cannot be claimed that the Morris and Philip Webb furniture shown at the beginning of this book is the source from which modern craft design springs, but these pieces as well as those by Lethaby and Voysey are of great historical interest and serve to mark the link with the Morris movement which this craft, as well as others, must acknowledge.

It can hardly be doubted that the strongest single influence upon the craft of furniture making in the early years of the century was the work of Ernest Gimson and the brothers Ernest and Sidney Barnsley. These three London architects were inspired by the work and ideals of William Morris. In 1893, after some valuable experience with a number of crafts in London, they went to the Cotswolds to learn and practise the crafts of building and principally, as it turned out, furniture making. In 1901 Peter Waals, a Dutch cabinet-maker, joined them to take charge of the workshops at Daneway House. In 1919, after Gimson's death, Peter Waals carried on the business at Chalford, where he became a very well-known figure in the craft world in the 1920's and 30's, a period when great interest was taken in craftsmanship, and in the craftsman by the discriminating public as well as in the educational world.

There are sufficient illustrations in this book of the work of what has since become known as the Cotswold school to give the reader a clear picture of the design of the Gimson-Barnsley-Waals furniture, though only the sight and feel of the work itself can reveal the perfection of its craftsmanship and the subtlety of its design. Let us not forget that all this, with the exception of the later Chalford work, is over 40 years old: it can easily be seen from these illustrations that Gimson and the Barnsleys turned their backs on everything which the furniture trade of their day was doing and went right back to the craft tradition of pre-industrial days, and from that starting point designed furniture for the needs of their own day.

The impact of this work from the Cotswolds upon the younger generation of craft workers and teachers in the years after the First World War went very deep, coming as it did at a time when the best that the furniture trade could offer was sham Jacobean and Sheraton, and when woodwork at school and college level, though long established, was in need of a new impetus and direction.

From the point of view of the craftsman, the design of the Cotswold work was a return to construction as the real foundation, as it had been to the makers of the simple furniture of the past—though not always to the 'great cabinet-makers'. On this foundation, they added subtle proportion and inventive decoration which was often itself part of the construction or served to emphasize construction. For example, the panelling of doors, a necessity when solid wood is used, is made into a distinctive decorative feature, and similarly with drawers and handles, stools, plinths and feet: none of these are disguised by the decorative treatment, but rather emphasized and their importance stressed. Another feature which should be noted is the use of the joints themselves as decorative features. But these are details which go to make up the whole: they do not altogether explain the artistry of the design which came in great variety from the Cotswold workshops.

Even in their own time, Gimson and his associates were not the only notable figures of the craft revival. A. Romney Green was an outstanding contemporary and he trained many pupils who are now well known. Sir Ambrose Heal was prominent as a designer and craftsman in the early years of the century, and in the years after the First World War Gordon Russell, today well known as Sir Gordon Russell, industrial designer and one-time Director of the Council of Industrial Design, was producing fine work of individual craftsmanship at his workshops at Broadway. Other well-known figures of the period up to 1939 were Edward Barnsley—son of Sidney Barnsley—who is today an outstanding designer, craftsman and college lecturer, and Stanley Davies who was making furniture at Windermere up to very recent times.

The later pages of this book show the work of craftsmen of our own time—teachers and students as well as professional designer-craftsmen in wood. The reader will see from these pages how the general look of the designs has been modified since the early Cotswold days. Modern craftsmen design for their own day, as Gimson designed for his. Today's homes generally require something a little lighter in appearance and construction. There are modern ideas, also, of the shape and style of furniture of which the craftsman must take account: but how far he should go along with 'contemporary' ideas which the public has absorbed from the furniture industry is a matter which each craftsman must settle for himself. Generally it would be true to say that the craftsman whose work is based on traditional methods and values approaches the new fashions launched upon the market with a critical and wary eye. The furniture trade is a mass-producing industry, at times using synthetic materials in place of natural woods, and having available new processes of assembly and finish, and with these the industrial designer is no longer bound by the restrictions of traditional construction. He is now free to experiment in ways which are not open to the hand craftsman, and almost anything is possible.

Obviously there comes a point where hand and machine must part company. It will be quite clear to anyone who follows the course of industrial design in furniture that eminent designers are now producing work with new materials and processes which is of high artistic quality in its own field but quite outside the craftsman's range. But within his range, the craftsman has to consider the impact of modern trends in design, and particularly the trend towards lightness and delicacy. In this connection it is interesting to compare the recent work of Edward Barnsley with the early work of the Cotswold school. A good designer-craftsman knows, through his understanding of his craft, what can properly be done, with reasonable economy of means, with the methods at his disposal. The public must not expect him to keep in step with every 'contemporary' fashion which may disappear as quickly as it has come. The restraint imposed by construction and other elements of what is loosely called 'tradition' is a kind of discipline which the craftsman accepts. Within this accepted limitation there is ample scope for originality, variety and the subtle touches of the designer-craftsman's personality. These are qualities which no mass-produced article can offer, and they are the qualities for which individual hand work is valued.

At one time it could have been said, with truth, that good workmanship and good design could be had from the hand craftsman and from him *alone*. This is no longer as true as it was, however, for the remarkable improvements seen in recent years in both the quality and the design of industrial products can be noted in furniture as well as in other household goods. But quality of workmanship is a matter of degree, and it is still true, and probably always will be true, that in the furniture-making craft the perfection of workmanship produced by a master craftsman using his traditional methods cannot be copied by machines. To take one example: a craftsman makes a drawer to fit perfectly into one place in an intended carcase; it runs smooth and true, and the construction of it combines strength with lightness. No machine can do this, nor ever will. The designer-craftsman handles wood as a live material. If he is a master of his craft and not prevented by economic considerations from doing his best work, a piece of furniture made by him will be of the best material in every part. There will be no inferior materials, or inferior workmanship in unseen parts, and construction will be the best which can be devised for the job. The final perfection of the workmanship will be seen in the fitting of the drawers and doors and in the care devoted to the finishing of the work. At one time, no doubt, work of this type could have been had from the furniture industry: today it comes from the small craft workshops, and from teachers and students.

Work of this quality and individuality takes time to produce and cannot be cheap to buy. Furniture making is a time-consuming fine craft even when the worker is highly skilled, and an individual piece made in a craftsman's workshop must be expensive when compared with a mass-produced article. The improvement in both design and quality of the higher-grade products of the furniture industry has greatly eroded the craftsman's potential market in recent years, but in spite of these difficulties the designer-craftsman maker of furniture still survives. He is in the happy position, in these days, of following a way of life which gives him contentment and satisfaction. He is not competing with the industrialists; he is not chasing higher output or engaging in sales promotion; his concern is to do good work and still live, but he cannot survive as a professional unless he can support himself by his work, and admittedly this is becoming more and more difficult. He deserves to be better known and supported, not only by private individuals who know good work when they see it and appreciate its qualities, but by industrial firms and public bodies. (In this connection, some of the new photographs shown in this book should prove interesting.) There is a great deal of modern woodwork in public places in this country, in churches great and small, for example, which falls far short of what a competent designer-craftsman could design and make if given the opportunity: which, alas, rarely happens. As for the private buyer, it is difficult to see why a man who can afford the best will furnish his house with reproduction 'antiques' when there are craftsmen ready to make for him individual pieces which will become treasured possessions not only for himself but for those who come after him. There would be many patrons of the 'fine crafts' if potential clients were more aware of the excellent workmanship which is available. One of the aims of the newly founded Crafts Council of Great Britain is to bring the crafts more to the notice of the general public and to put craftsmen in touch with those who would enjoy possessing fine work.

There are, of course, very many designer-craftsmen in wood in this country whose work is not offered for sale and does not commonly appear at craft exhibitions. These are—not exclusively but in large measure—handicraft teachers, and the staffs and students of colleges where craft teachers are trained. Between these teacher-craftsmen and the professionals working in craft workshops there is a close affinity, for they come under the same influences, and the style and character of their work is very similar. Many craftsmen now practising in their own workshops learnt their craft in the course of their training as teachers, and many of them combine their craft work with teaching. Eminent professional designer-craftsmen lecture and demonstrate and advise in teacher training colleges, and the students from the colleges become in due course practising craftsmen themselves, though not necessarily professional ones. The illustrations at the end of this book show but a few examples of the large body of similar work produced every year by men who will pass out to be teachers of craft in secondary schools of all types. As craftsmen they will work largely for themselves, but collectively they account for a great deal in any assessment of the place of the designer-craftsman in wood in this country today.

The English are, in a sense, a nation of woodworkers. Woodwork has been taught in English schools for over half a century: today most English boys leave school with a working knowledge of elementary woodwork, and a large proportion of them have begun to master the early stages of craft woodwork of a kind which would lead them, if continued, to furniture making in the fine craftsman's manner. Some continue—how many cannot even be guessed at. There are, of course, serious obstacles for most people who try to reach out beyond 'do-it-yourself' techniques and follow the craft in the craftsman's way. Serious woodwork is no kitchen-table craft: it necessitates considerable tool equipment, and space which few modern homes can provide. Some overcome the obstacles at home, some by attendance at evening classes, and many more would do so if there were some place where they could get workshop space. If the community could provide this (perhaps in Community Centres?) the numbers of serious amateur craftsmen emerging might be dramatic. In these days of ever-increasing leisure, this craft, learnt properly and practised seriously, could become an occupation of absorbing interest and could lead many people to experience the satisfaction which the expert and practised craftsman feels in producing something of the highest possible standards of workmanship and worthy to be called a work of art. There is no need today for the amateur who wishes to improve his work to be taken in by the cheap and nasty workmanship and design which is offered to him by some people: there is plenty of good work to inspire him, and a good selection of it is shown in this book.

The illustrations included here have been made as representative as possible, but suitable photographs were not available for everything that the author would have wished to show. The wood sculptures and wood turnings are included because the makers, when considering a design and its execution, appear to have appreciated the use of wood as a live material responsive to climatic changes, and to have overcome the difficulties imposed by the grain. The reader will see that this book includes none of the objects described by Herbert Read (in *Modern Sculpture*) as 'those "assemblages" of diverse ready-made objects designed to amuse or shock rather than to create any aesthetic emotion'. The sculptures and turnings shown here are complementary to the furniture because they exhibit further evidence of the existence today of woodwork as a fine craft.

The author hopes that these photographs and the story they illustrate will interest not only actual and aspiring designer-craftsmen, but also a much larger public whose support is necessary if the fine crafts are to survive.

March 1965

WILLIAM MORRIS (1834–96)

Room in Kelmscott Manor near Lechlade, the country
home of William Morris from 1871 until his
death in 1896 and now the property of Oxford
University. Table and settle designed by William Morris
and Philip Webb.

WILLIAM MORRIS

Painted chest by William Morris and Philip Webb.

W. R. Lethaby was an architect, author, art historian, designer, and an associate of William Morris. He became the first principal of the L.C.C. Central School of Arts and Crafts in 1896 and in 1916 he was appointed surveyor of the fabric at Westminster Abbey.

The upper photograph on the opposite page shows a sideboard in oak, carved and with inlaid doors, designed by Lethaby in 1900.

C. F. A. Voysey was a brilliant architect and designer. His designs exerted a great influence for many years because, in contrast to the prevailing trends, they were simple and unaffected.

The lower illustration opposite shows the living room and furniture at The Orchard, Chorley Wood, designed in 1899.

W. R. LETHABY (1857–1931)

C. F. A. VOYSEY (1857–1941)

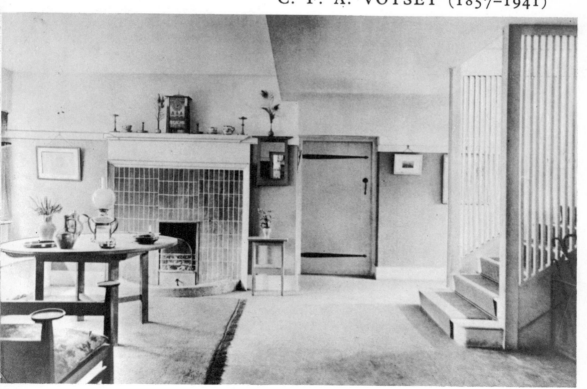

3

SIR AMBROSE HEAL (1872–1959)

On leaving Marlborough College Ambrose Heal was apprenticed to a cabinet-maker, and made a special study of furniture before joining the family business. A first-rate craftsman, with the originality of the true artist, his designs for both hand-made and machine-made furniture had a far-reaching influence on present-day furnishing trends. He was one of the founders of the Design and Industries Association.

The photographs on pages 4 to 6 show furniture designed by Ambrose Heal for Heal and Son between 1900 and 1932. Actual dates are given when known.

Bureau bookcase in unpolished oak: about 1900.

Dresser in unpolished oak (width 48 in.), with two small drawers, one large drawer and two cup- boards, and a plate rack (42 in. wide) to match: 1905.

Dresser in unpolished
oak: 1914.

Walnut sideboard with
fitments for bottles
and cutlery: 1930.

Bookcase in Queensland walnut, for the boardroom of the Westminster Bank: 1930.

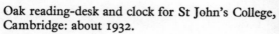

Oak reading-desk and clock for St John's College, Cambridge: about 1932.

ERNEST GIMSON (1864–1919)

The photographs on pages 7 to 15 show a selection
of the work designed by Gimson and made in
his workshops at Daneway House. The date of the
piece and the name of the craftsman are given
where known.

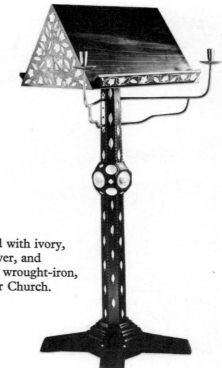

Lectern in ebony, inlaid with ivory,
mother-of-pearl and silver, and
candlesticks of polished wrought-iron,
made in 1906, for Roker Church.

Chest in English walnut, inlaid with
darker walnut and cherry, and with hand-
made brass drawer-handles, on a stand of
English walnut. Made by Peter Waals.

The Gimson Room, Sapperton,
Gloucestershire.

Dresser in English oak.

ERNEST GIMSON

Armchair (height 41 in.), in English
walnut, with ebony reed inlay, made in 1926
by P. H. W. Burchett in the workshops of
Peter Waals.

Two chairs, in English walnut, with inlay
and rush seats, made by P. H. W. Burchett.

Octagonal dining-table, in English walnut,
made by H. Davoll.

Expanding dining-table, with inlay of holly
and ebony, made by H. Davoll.

Walnut writing-desk made
by Fred Gardiner.

Chest of drawers and small
cabinet.

Sideboard in English walnut, with brass
handles, a pair of wrought-iron candlesticks
and a walnut glove-box, all designed by
Gimson. The sideboard was made by
H. Davoll.

Walnut cabinet, made by Ernest Smith:
about 1917.

Mahogany writing-cabinet,
made by Ernest Smith.

Writing-cabinet, partly veneered with burr-elm and ebony, and a box in English walnut inlaid with mother-of-pearl.

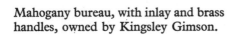

Mahogany bureau, with inlay and brass handles, owned by Kingsley Gimson.

ERNEST BARNSLEY (1861–1926)

Gate-leg table: 1907.

The photographs on pages 17 to 21 show a selection of the work designed by Sidney Barnsley. The date and name of the craftsman are given when known.

SIDNEY BARNSLEY (1863–1926)

Oak sideboard owned
by W. G. Simmonds.

Oak sideboard (height 72 in.,
length 84 in., width 30 in.),
made in 1900 and now
owned by Edward Barnsley.

Lectern (height 58 in.) in English oak inlaid with
mother-of-pearl, ebony and holly: 1902.

Cabinet: about 1910.

SIDNEY BARNSLEY

Walnut cabinet (height 49 in.) on stand,
made about 1910, for the late St John
Hornby, Esq. (Reproduced by kind permission
of *Country Life*.)

Interior of the same cabinet. The painted
decoration, executed in 1913, is by Louise
Powell.

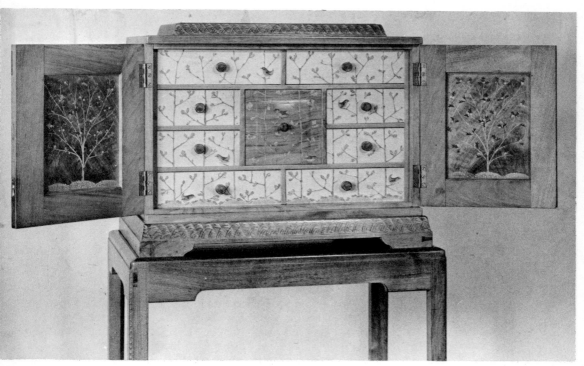

Oak sideboard fixture, in a panelled recess in a
dining-room at Rodmarton, Gloucestershire, designed
by Sidney Barnsley and made by A. Wright in 1926.
This fixture is in a Cotswold house designed by
Ernest Barnsley for the Hon. Claud Biddulph, and
built by local masons from materials on the estate.

Chest (height 27 in., width 52 in., depth 25 in.) in
English oak, with domed top and wrought-iron hinges.

Oak table made in 1927 by Walter Berry in Edward
Barnsley's workshop, Froxfield, Hants. This table is
at Rodmarton, Gloucestershire.

PETER WAALS (1865–1937)

On the death of Gimson, Peter Waals, his manager since 1901, decided to set up new workshops with a number of the craftsmen who were still alive. This he did in 1920 in Chalford, Gloucestershire, with much success.

The photographs on pages 22 to 27 show a selection of the work designed by Waals and made under his direction. The date of the piece and the name of the craftsman are given when known.

Newspaper rack (height 13 in., width 15 in.), in English walnut designed by Peter Waals.

Two views of Peter Waals's workshops at Chalford (1920–37).
The upper photograph opposite shows Ernest Smith in the foreground and H. Davoll behind him.
  The lower photograph opposite shows Percy Burchett in the foreground, and at the back without apron is Peter Waals.

Bedside cupboard (height 28 in., width 15 in., depth 15 in.), in English walnut, designed by Peter Waals.

English walnut cabinet (height 63 in., width 39 in., depth 18 in.), with hand-made brass locks designed by Gimson and made by Peter Waals in 1921.

English walnut writing-cabinet (height 50 in., width 44 in., depth 18 in.), with drop front and inlay of stringed ebony and holly, designed by Gimson and made for the Wembley Exhibition, 1924.

PETER WAALS

Small cabinet, in walnut made
by P. H. W. Burchett.

Sideboard (height 35 in., length 72 in., depth
19 in.), in walnut, designed by Gimson and
made in 1928.

Oak armchair made
by Owen Scrubey.

Oak chair made
by Ernest Smith.

PETER WAALS

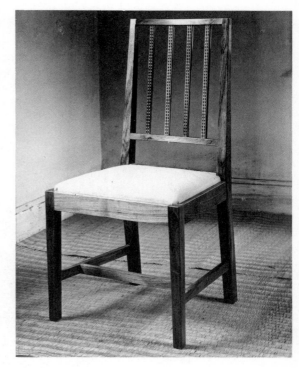

Dining-chair, with inlay,
made by P. H. W. Burchett.

Casket in Macassar ebony (length 10 in., width and height $5\frac{1}{2}$ in.).
The base and lip mouldings are of black ebony; the interior has a
cedar lining, $\frac{1}{8}$ in. thick, which is dovetailed at the corners; top
and bottom are grooved into the sides. The casket, which was
exhibited at an Arts and Crafts Exhibition at the Royal Academy,
was designed by Peter Waals, and made by E. A. Drake when a
student at Loughborough Training College in 1938. (Mr Drake
is now a Senior Lecturer at the College.)

SIR GORDON RUSSELL (born 1892)

The photographs on pages 28 to 31 are examples of the handmade furniture designed by Gordon Russell and made in the Russell workshops at Broadway at various dates between 1920 and 1930. Sir Gordon Russell's distinguished work as industrial designer and as Director of the Council of Industrial Design is outside the scope of this book.

Mirror (height 31 in., width 23 in., depth 9½ in.) in walnut frame, made in 1924 by Edgar Turner, with metalwork by S. H. Gardiner.

Oak table (diameter 36 in.)

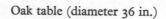

Chairs in English walnut inlaid with ebony and
yew-tree, made by C. Turner.

Sideboard in English walnut, inlaid with ebony and
yew-tree, made by F. Shilton.

Cabinet on stand, in English walnut inlaid with ebony, box and laburnum, exhibited in Paris, 1925, and awarded a gold medal. It was made in 1924 by W. Marks.

GORDON RUSSELL

Cabinet in walnut and ebony, with
drawer-handles of ebony and box,
designed for exhibition in the Palace of
Arts, Wembley, and made in 1924 by
Edgar Turner, with metalwork by
S. H. Gardiner.

EDWARD BARNSLEY, C.B.E.
(born 1900)

Edward Barnsley, is pre-eminent as a
designer, craftsman and teacher. He has
his own workshop with pupil-apprentices;
he has assisted associations such as the
Rural Industries Bureau; and he is
Adviser in Woodwork Design to
Loughborough Training College for
Teachers. Believing that a craftsman
should, if an opportunity arises, design
work for making outside his workshop,
he has put his belief into practice by
designing work for the University College
of Ghana.

The photographs on pages 32 to 35
show a selection of the work designed by
Edward Barnsley.

Chest of drawers
(length 37 in.), in
makore, made by
Oskar Dawson in 1954.

Dining table (length 108 in., width 36 in.), in blackbean,
with laminated stretcher rail, made by Alan Balcombe in 1964.

Cabinet (height 72 in., width 36 in.),
in English walnut, with shaped glass
by Hudsons, Glass Benders of London,
made by George Taylor.

Master's Parlour Furniture, in walnut,
made for the Carpenters' Company,
Carpenters Hall, London, E.C.2,
in 1959.

Side table (length 72 in.), in walnut,
made by Alan Balcombe in 1964.

Dining-room table (length 120 in.,
width 42 in.) and chairs, in
rosewood, for Messrs. Courtaulds
Directors' Small Dining Room,
18 Hanover Square, London, W.1
made by Herbert Upton, George
Taylor and Oskar Dawson in 1964.

A. ROMNEY GREEN (1872–1945)

A. Romney Green was sailor, poet, teacher, mathematician and craftsman. He broadcast, contributed to yachting journals, and wrote a book entitled *Woodwork in Principle and Practice*. After he had given up teaching, he lived by constructing furniture, which he exhibited at the Arts and Crafts Exhibition Society and at international exhibitions in Paris, Milan and St Louis.

Photograph cabinet (height 48 in., width 30 in., depth 16 in.), in Cuban mahogany inlaid with ebony and box, owned by J. C. Thomson.

Mahogany armchair, owned by J. C.
Thomson.

Cabinet (height 56 in., width 32 in.,
depth 20 in.) in walnut, inlaid with ebony
and walnut, owned by J. C. Thomson.

STANLEY W. DAVIES (born 1894)

Stanley W. Davies is a graduate of Oxford University who came under the influence of the late A. Romney Green and has been designing and making furniture for many years. His work has been widely exhibited, and his workshop at Windermere is well known.

Prayer desk in oak (width 27 in., depth 25½ in., height 39½ in.).

Oak armchair (height overall 40¼ in., seat 21 in. and 17 in. × 17 in. × 17½ in. high).

Indian laurel-wood cabinet (width 34 in., depth 13 in., height 53¾ in.).

Walnut corner cupboard (length 18 in., width 18 in., height 33 in.).

ERIC SHARPE (born 1888)

Eric Sharpe was a pupil of A. Romney Green for eight years and, later, became a designer-craftsman working on his own account. He has been responsible for many important pieces of work, including the casket presented by the Corporation of London to the Prime Minister (the Rt. Hon. (Sir) Winston Spencer Churchill) in 1943.

The Swan Chair, in walnut inlaid with holly and ebony, and carved, made in 1943.

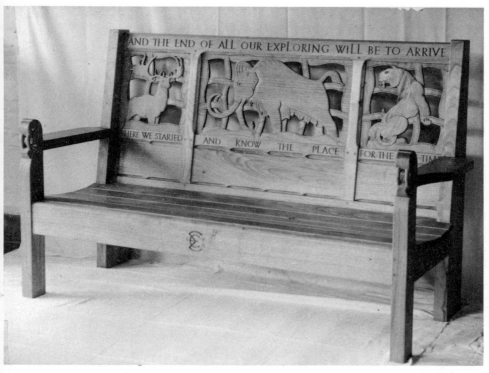

Settle (length 60 in.), in chestnut, designed and made in 1955. The carved and pierced panels depict Irish deer, a mammoth and a sabre-toothed tiger, and the inscription is a quotation from T. S. Eliot.

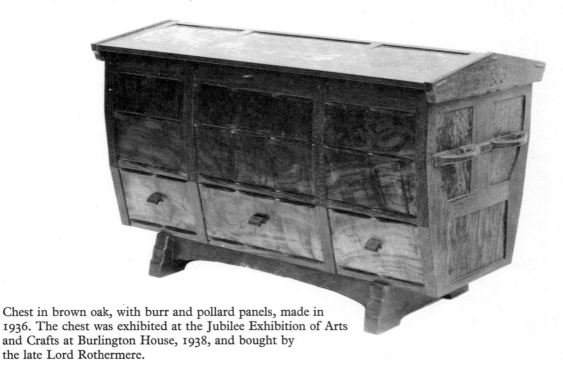

Chest in brown oak, with burr and pollard panels, made in 1936. The chest was exhibited at the Jubilee Exhibition of Arts and Crafts at Burlington House, 1938, and bought by the late Lord Rothermere.

SIR GEORGE L. TREVELYAN (born 1906)

Sir George L. Trevelyan, Bart., M.A. has been Warden of Shropshire Adult College, Attingham Park, Shrewsbury, since 1947. A former teacher at Gordonstoun School, during 1930–31 he worked as an artist-craftsman with Peter Waals, in the Chalford workshops. He has lectured on hand-made furniture for the Council of Industrial Design.

Chair, in walnut inlaid with holly, designed and owned by Sir George L. Trevelyan, and made by Ernest Smith in 1949.

Walnut desk and chairs in The Adult College, Attingham Park, Shropshire. The desk was made in 1949 by Ernest Smith to Sir George L. Trevelyan's design. The chairs were made in 1931 to Gimson designs, the one on the left by P. H. W. Burchett and the one on the right by Sir George L. Trevelyan.

A. GREGORY (1888–1963)

A. Gregory, a member of the Royal Birmingham Society of Artists, also a silver medallist of the City & Guilds of London Institute, served an apprenticeship to cabinet-making and trained at Shoreditch Training College to become a teacher. After gaining experience in London schools, he became the Head of the School of Furniture and Handicraft Teachers' Training Department at the Birmingham College of Arts and Crafts from 1923 to 1953. He was the author of well-known books on woodwork.

Walnut Secretaire.

Sideboard (length 48 in.,
height 36 in.), in solid
walnut, with veneered
fronts, made in 1936.

Altar and communion rails (length 52 in., height 37 in.) in oak,
centre panel motif in gold leaf, made in 1948.

H. DAVOLL (1875–1963)

H. Davoll served an apprenticeship in Hereford, spent some years in Liverpool,
and then assisted Ernest Gimson, at Daneway, from 1901–19. He then went with Peter
Waals to Chalford where he stayed until 1933, when he started his own workshop.

Writing-desk in walnut, octagonal in plan (length 42 in.
width 21 in., table height 29 in., total height 35⅜ in.),
made in 1941, and owned by the British Council, London.

Walnut sideboard
(height 36 in., width
45 in., depth 21 in.),
designed and made by
H. Davoll in 1948.

F. P. GARDINER (1889–1961)

F. P. Gardiner served an apprenticeship to woodworking, then worked for
thirteen years with Ernest Gimson, and five years with Peter Waals.

Sideboard (length 78 in., width
20 in., height 36 in.), made
in 1954.

ROBIN NANCE (born 1907)

Robin Nance was trained by the late A. Romney Green. He started his own
workshops in 1933, at St Ives, with the object of producing mainly by hand (using
machines only in the early stages of the work), well-designed furniture within the reach of
people of modest means. He usually employs four to six craftsmen, and sometimes under-
takes architect-designed work.

Knock-down furniture made
in 1958. The magazine
rack (length 16 in.,
width 11 in., height 12 in.)
is veneered on tempered
hardboard. The pack-flat
table is 36 in. long, 14 in.
wide and 14 in. high.

Table, in teak (top
72 in. × 42 in. open,
height 29 in.) designed
in 1960.

Corner cupboard (width
28 in., depth 17 in., height
38 in.) in African Walnut,
made in 1956.

Sapele chairs (seat height 17 in., total
height 51 in. Seat size 18 in. front;
13 in. back; 15 in. from front to back),
made in 1960.

JUDITH E. HUGHES

Miss Judith E. Hughes has her own workshop at Tavistock, Devon, where she produces fine furniture and marquetry. Her work has been shown at many exhibitions and she is a member of the Devon Guild of Craftsmen.

Coffee table (length $19\frac{1}{4}$ in., width 12 in., height 20 in.), veneered English walnut, made in 1951, and exhibited in Florence, in 1952, by the Arts and Crafts Exhibition Society. The top of the table is hinged, to allow access to the workbox, the interior of which is veneered in figured English sycamore.

Table (length 72 in., width 28 in., height 30 in.), in Burma teak, ebony feet and line. Marquetry coat of arms in walnut, sycamore, satinwood, birch, ebony and Thuya burr, made in 1963.

JOHN BRIGGS (1911–64)

John Briggs spent many years making furniture and turning in wood. From 1932–3 he studied with Edward Barnsley.

Cross (height 9 in.), in English walnut inlaid with holly. The ring is also holly.

Bow-fronted corner cupboard (height 21½ in., width 20 in.), in Muninga.

W. R. BURDEN (1885-1957)

W. R. Burden was a founder member of the Sandon Studios Society of Liverpool, and a teacher of cabinet-making at the Liverpool College of Art.

Walnut tallboy (height 60 in., width 33 in., depth 20 in.), made in 1950.

ALLAN SMITH (born 1908)

Allan Smith was apprenticed to a cabinet-maker in Burnley. He joined the staff of the Rural Industries Bureau in 1948 and assisted in establishing the workshops at Wimbledon, where he came under the influence of Edward Barnsley. Allan Smith is now a technical officer with the Furniture Development Council.

Chest, in plane (length 38½ in., depth 19½ in., height 22 in.),
made at the furniture workshops of the Rural Industries Bureau, 1949.

THEO. A. DALRYMPLE (born 1912)

Theo. A. Dalrymple received his early training
in a small hand-workshop in Surrey. He
started designing and making original furniture
in 1946, and set up his present workshop in 1948.
A craft member of several national craft societies,
his output includes furniture for homes,
churches and cottages. He likes to use naturally-
seasoned English hardwoods, but also uses the
traditional imported woods.

Mahogany dining-chair (height:
back 36 in., front 17 in., width at front
21 in.), made in 1955.

A. J. EVES (born 1913)

A. J. Eves, B.A., is a Training College lecturer who specializes in craftwork.
He is a member of the Society of Industrial Artists, The Crafts Council of Great Britain
and the Society of Designer Craftsmen.

Magazine table (length
54 in., width 18 in.,
height 16 in.) in beech
and teak, made in
1956, for a doctor's
waiting-room.

Occasional table (length 32 in., width 18 in., height 16 in.)
in French walnut and sycamore, made in 1955, and
included that year in the Arts Council of Great Britain
Travelling Exhibition.

Plant table (length 32 in., width 16 in., height 20 in.),
in English oak and Australian walnut, made in 1954.

E. J. RICE (born 1914)

E. J. Rice was trained at Loughborough Training College and Birmingham College of Art, and is now the principal of the Lydney School of Art. As a member of the Guild of Gloucestershire Craftsmen he still continues to design and construct furniture.

Chest, in English walnut, made in 1941.

Church furniture, in oak, made in 1951.

ROBERT TOWNSHEND (born 1917)

Robert Townshend studied at the L.C.C. Central School of Arts and Crafts. He was a pupil of Edward Barnsley for two years and then opened his present workshop at Middleton, Saxmundham. In 1952 he won a joint First Prize in the Rural Industries Bureau's furniture design competition.

Writing-table (length 45 in., width $22\frac{1}{2}$ in., height $28\frac{1}{2}$ in.), in walnut, with inlaid ebony, made in 1962.

Bureau (length 36 in., width $18\frac{1}{2}$ in., height $39\frac{1}{2}$ in.), in English walnut, with inlaid ebony, and interior parts of cedar, made in 1962.

HUGH BIRKETT (born 1919)

Hugh Birkett, once a pupil of Oliver Morel, now has his own workshop in which he designs and makes domestic and church furniture. He is a member of the Red Rose Guild of Craftsmen, the Arts and Crafts Exhibition Society, and The Crafts Centre of Great Britain.

Walnut cabinet (width 37 in., depth 14 in., height 70 in.), designed and made by Hugh Birkett in 1957. The cabinet is now in the possession of Stoke-on-Trent College of Art

OLIVER MOREL (born 1916)

Oliver Morel studied and worked with Edward Barnsley from 1934 to 1941, except for an interval of teaching. He began in his own workshop in 1946, combining his work there with a smallholding. He is now settled in Herefordshire. Examples of his work are shown on pages 59–61.

Fitted sideboard (length 63 in.), in English walnut, made in 1957.

Lectern in oak, with swivel top, made in 1955.

Corner cupboard (height 36 in.), in old oak, made in 1953.

Small chest of drawers (length 39 in.), in brown oak, made in 1955.

KENNETH D. LAMPARD (born 1926)

Kenneth D. Lampard was elected a Member of the Arts and Crafts Exhibition Society in 1948 and has exhibited at The Crafts Centre of Great Britain since 1950.

Dining-chair, in walnut, with the back inlaid with rosewood, made in 1952.

Walnut work-table (length 20 in., width 12 in.,
height 23 in.), made in 1953. It consists of a
table combined with a sewing-box lined
in English plane, with handles forged in
gilding metal.

KENNETH MARSHALL (born 1923)

Kenneth Marshall was a pupil of Edward Barnsley. He started his own workshop in 1950, and is a member of the Guild of Gloucestershire Craftsmen.

Mahogany dressing-table (length 34 in., width 17 in., height 30½ in.), made in 1956, after modifications by Edward Barnsley.

Chair (height 36 in., width 24 in.), in English oak, with wool rep upholstery, made in 1954.

H. S. SWANN (born 1925)

H. S. Swann was trained by the Architectural Association from 1947–50. He started the business of designing and making furniture in 1950, and has since been responsible for much successful work, including church work, of a simple unadorned character.

Altar cross (height 36 in.)
of sycamore inlaid with yew,
at Ashington Parish
Church, made in 1951.

A. VERA SIMPSON

Miss A. Vera Simpson of Liverpool is a designer-craftswoman who studied various aspects of art, including painting and engraving, before concentrating on the designing and making of furniture. For a time she was a student of the late W. R. Burden, and now has her own workshop in which she produces well-made and attractive furniture that has been accepted by the Society of Designer Craftsmen and for the Red Rose Guild Exhibitions.

Sideboard (length 60 in.) in English walnut, with break front, centre bowed.

Side table (length 36 in.) in English walnut.

EDWARD BALY (born 1903)

Edward Baly was a research chemist with I.C.I. until the outbreak of the war, after which he trained as a cabinet-maker starting his own workshop in 1950. He is a founder-member of the Devon Guild of Craftsmen, and a member of the Red Rose Guild of Craftsmen and The Crafts Centre of Great Britain.

Special version of a coffee table (length 39 in., width 16 in., height 16 in.), made in 1954, for a timber merchant to display samples of exotic woods. The star shows 32 different woods from Australia and New Zealand.

Dining table (48 in. dia.) in yew, yew veneers and solid octagonal inlay in beech.

KEITH COOPER (born 1917)

A law student before the Second World War, after which he became a pupil of Richard Coghlan of Harrogate, Keith Cooper started his own workshop in 1949. A full member of the Red Rose Guild of Craftsmen and The Crafts Centre of Great Britain, he specializes in church, school and domestic furniture, and letter-cutting.

Writing-table (length 38 in., width 18 in., height 30 in.) in Afrormosia inlaid with boxwood, and with two drawers, made in 1958. Note the sloping rail, and chamferred rail at the bottom.

Typewriting table without drawers, and free-standing desk with drawers, in American walnut inlaid with box-wood, made in 1957. The table is 39 in. long, 20 in. wide and 28½ in. high.

ALEC McCURDY (born 1914)

Alec McCurdy was a solicitor with the Westmorland County Council until he worked as a pupil with Stanley Davies and later with Edward Barnsley. He now works on his own using mainly English timbers. On his work he carves 'AM', the date, and a leaf of the appropriate timber.

Cherry work-table inlaid with holly, and
pin-box and button-tray in sycamore,
made in 1956.

Armchair, in oak and walnut, made in 1958.

Corner cabinet, in walnut inlaid with holly and cherry, and with shelves of sycamore, made in 1958.

ARTHUR B. REYNOLDS (1904–61)

A skilled craftsman in wood who was influenced by the work of Ernest Gimson, Arthur B. Reynolds worked for some years with Stanley Davies of Windermere, and eventually established the business in Ludlow which is now controlled by his two sons.

Buffet or sideboard (length 37 in., width 18½ in., height 54 in.) in cherry, with one full shelf and one shaped half-shelf adjustable, made in 1958.

Walnut side table
designed in 1954.

R. H. FYSON (born 1917)

R. H. Fyson entered the Royal Navy as a cadet in 1935. He retired, with the rank
Lieutenant-Commander, to take up professional woodworking in 1949, since when he has
produced a variety of beautiful work. He is now receiving many commissions for
ecclesiastical work.

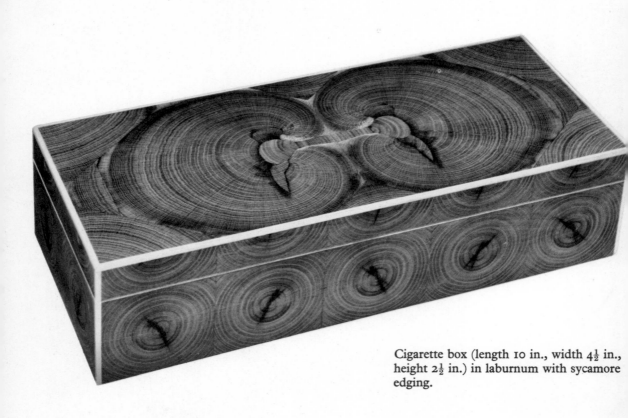

Cigarette box (length 10 in., width 4½ in.,
height 2½ in.) in laburnum with sycamore
edging.

Stationery cabinet (length 21 in., width 8 in., height 13 in.). Main carcase in African walnut; flanking pieces to tambours in beech; plinth veneered in Macassar ebony; drawer fronts in sycamore. Made in 1960 for Member of College of Handicraft Examination.

G. NIXON ALDERSLEY (born 1923)

G. Nixon Aldersley trained as a handicraft teacher after the war, and came under the influence of Edward Barnsley at Loughborough College. Work designed and executed by him was first exhibited at the Red Rose Guild of Craftsmen in 1949, and at The Crafts Centre of Great Britain in 1954.

Writing-table (length 40 in., width 18 in., height 30 in.), in American black walnut with holly inlay, purchased by Manchester City Art Gallery in 1957.

Two-seat hall chair, in Honduras mahogany.

Book ends, in English walnut, with ebony and box inlay. Turned powder bowls, in mahogany, with teak lids and purple heart knobs. Table lamp, in teak, with box and purple heart inlay.

Bedside table, in American black walnut, with tiles by Leo Matthews. The tiles on the front are enclosed in a cock bead.

H. R. HENSTOCK and
G. W. HINES

Oak lectern (height 40½ in., width 20 in., depth 14 in.) for Calder High School, Mytholmroyd, designed and made by H. R. Henstock and G. W. Hines who are masters at the school.

GWYN HUGHES

Gwyn Hughes came under the influence of Edward Barnsley while he was a student at Loughborough Training College for Teachers. He is a member of the Red Rose Guild of Craftsmen.

Bardic Chair (total height 49½ in., seat height 18 in.), designed and made for the Royal National Eisteddfod of Wales (Caernarvon, 1959). The chair is in oak and has a modelled red dragon on the back of the natural English calf upholstery.

IEUAN OWEN

Ieuan Owen is H.M. Inspector of Schools, furniture designer, craftsman, musician and former teacher.

Clavichord (length 45 in., width 18 in., height 30 in.), casework—English cherry; legs —rounded, square-sectioned aluminium; white keys—fiddle rib sycamore; dark keys— English walnut; tangents— carved from English lime; sound board—fine grained white pine; bridge—steam bent beach; top—lipped and veneered laminboard.

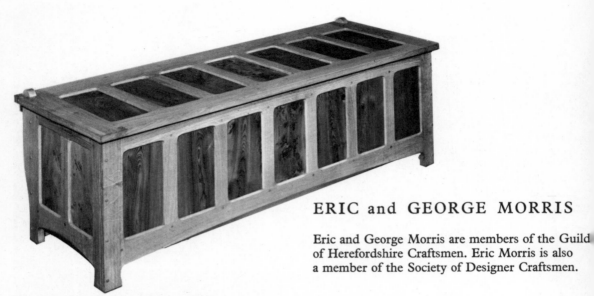

ERIC and GEORGE MORRIS

Eric and George Morris are members of the Guild of Herefordshire Craftsmen. Eric Morris is also a member of the Society of Designer Craftsmen.

Long chest (length 64 in., width 23 in., height 20 in.), in Evesbatch Court Estate oak and yew, made in The Craft Workshop at Evesbatch Court, Bishops Frome, home of W. David Porter, Esq.

R. A. N. MACKILLIGIN

R. A. N. Mackilligin trained with Edward Barnsley and he has also studied and worked in Denmark.

High chair, in Rio rosewood, Lebanon cedar and green leather. For Bishop Otter College, Chichester.

ERNEST JOYCE

Ernest Joyce has made furniture for royalty, universities, cathedrals and private customers. He is now part-time Head of Furniture Department at Brighton College of Art.

Cocktail cabinet (height 48 in., width 30 in., depth 18 in.), in walnut, interiors lined with pear wood, made in 1959.

Furniture made by students in Training Colleges is shown on pages 82 to 95.
The illustrations in this section are but a few examples of the large quantity of fine furniture
made every year in the colleges by prospective handicraft teachers as part of their course.

Table (length 38¾ in.,
width 20 in., height
29 in.), in English walnut
and cherry with hand-
made brass handles,
made in 1963 by a
student at Redland
College, Bristol.

Table (length 40 in., width 18 in.,
height 30 in.), in teak, made in
1961 by a student at The College,
Chester.

Easy chair, in teak, with black leather upholstered Fibreglass shell, made in 1962 by a student at Goldsmiths' College.

Dining-table in sapele by E. SMITH, needlework cabinet with tambour top in Australian walnut by C. C. BIRD, dressing-table veneered in Australian walnut by R. H. STOKES: all students of Goldsmiths' College in 1955.

Side table (length 54 in.,
width 18 in., height 32 in.)
in Cuban mahogany with
inlaid holly lines; weathered
sycamore drawer fronts; and
stainless steel handles. The
end rails, which are of
'sandwich' construction
(six layers of $\frac{3}{16}$ in.
mahogany), are joined to
each leg with two cross-
grained tongues. The top
is secret lap dovetailed on
to the ends. Made by
A. PETERS at Shoreditch
Training College in 1959.

Jewel casket (length 7½ in., width 4½ in., height 3 in.) in Cuban mahogany inlaid with ivory; ebony feet; and ebony and holly handle. The interior is lined with English yew and royal purple velvet. The casket was presented to H.M. Queen Elizabeth II at the Education and Careers Exhibition in 1959. Made by A. PETERS, with hand-made silver keys by R. HOSKIN, at Shoreditch Training College.

Room dividers (height 72 in., width 39 in., depth 16 in. approximately). Left: in teak and Brazilian rosewood. Right: in teak. Made by students at Shoreditch Training College.

Small sewing-cabinets in English walnut. Left: by
G. W. BROOKS. Right: by R. J. LARGE. Both were
made at Loughborough Training College in 1954.

English walnut bow-fronted sideboard (length 48 in.
width 16 in., height 36 in.), made by A. DICKENSON,
Loughborough Training College in 1959.

Table (length 72 in.), in English oak, carefully selected and curved, made by a student at Loughborough Training College, in 1964.

Record player (length 34 in., width 15 in., height 32 in.) in sapele, made by
K. N. HINCHCLIFFE, Shoreditch Training College, in 1960.

Workbox (length 20 in., width 12 in., height 26 in.), in blackbean, made by a student at Loughborough Training College, in 1963.

Display cabinet (length 30 in., width 13 in., height 48 in.) in sapele and sycamore, made by D. A. ROBINSON, Loughborough Training College, in 1960.

Sideboard (length 58 in., width 19 in., height 34 in.) in sapele, with rosewood drawer fronts, door frames and stringing, and knobs of brass and rosewood, made by D. P. CRAVEN, Loughborough Training College, in 1959.

Lectern (height 36 in., top 27 in. by 20 in.) for College Hall, in makore, made by students at Cheshire County Training College, Alsager, in 1964.

Table (length 84 in., width 30 in., height 30 in.) for the College Hall, in makore, made by students at Cheshire County Training College, Alsager, in 1964.

Cabinet with glass in doors, and two drawers in walnut and sycamore, made by a student at Shoreditch Training College.

Bow-fronted table in walnut, with three drawers, made by a student at Shoreditch Training College.

Table with glass top
(length 48 in.,
width 15 in., height
15 in.) in rosewood,
made by
A. BENHAM,
Shoreditch Training
College, in 1960.

Sideboard (length 52 in., width 18 in., height 34 in.) in sapele with
rosewood handles, made by C. F. WILLETTS, Shoreditch Training
College, in 1959.

These two pages show work by students of the College of Art and Industrial Design, Newcastle-upon-Tyne.

Combined writing/dressing-table (length 36 in., depth 19 in., height 30 in.), in American black walnut and white ash. The lid on the right slides. Made by a student.

Prie-dieu (width 35 in., depth 24½ in., height 32½ in.), main laminated structure in Honduras mahogany, with insert block of multi-plywood, faced on either side with Bombay rosewood. Reading rest in solid Bombay rosewood. Made by a student.

WOOD SCULPTURE AND WOOD TURNINGS

The illustrations in this section are but a few examples of the large quantity of handmade work of this category.

W. G. SIMMONDS

After studying wood-carving and sculpture at the Royal College of Art and the Royal Academy School, W. G. Simmonds assisted Edwin Abbey, R.A., with the mural decorations for the Pennsylvania State Capital. He moved to Far Oakridge, Gloucestershire, in 1919, since when, in addition to wood-carving and sculpture, he has widened his interests to include drama and puppetry.

'Five Little Pigs' in sycamore (length 11 in., width 7 in., height 6 in.), exhibited in the Royal Academy Summer Exhibition, 1959.

'Autumn Calf' in painted oak (length 18 in., width 16 in.,
height 9 in.), made in 1952, and now in the permanent collection of the
Cheltenham Art Gallery and Museum.

'The Farm Team' in elm (length 60 in., height 18 in.), made in 1928,
and owned by the Tate Gallery.
(Reproduced by courtesy of the Tate Gallery.)

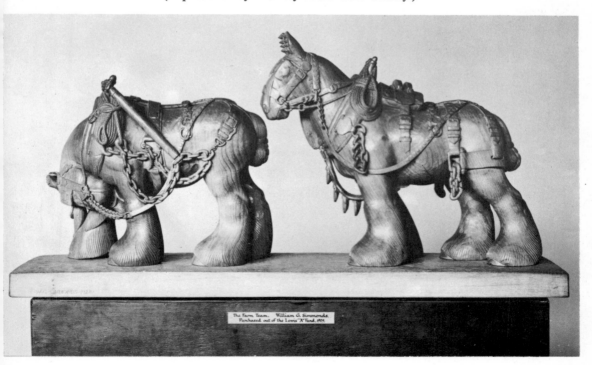

S. M. and MICHAEL S. TURNER

These craftsmen are the second and third generations of a family of cabinet-makers and wood-carvers.

Font cover, in English oak, with a leaf-gold cross, made in 1953.

Crucifix (height 54 in.) in English elm, made in 1959 by
Ray Arnatt, a third-year student at the Royal College of Art.
The crucifix was commissioned by one of the Borstal
Institutions.

MEG RUTHERFORD

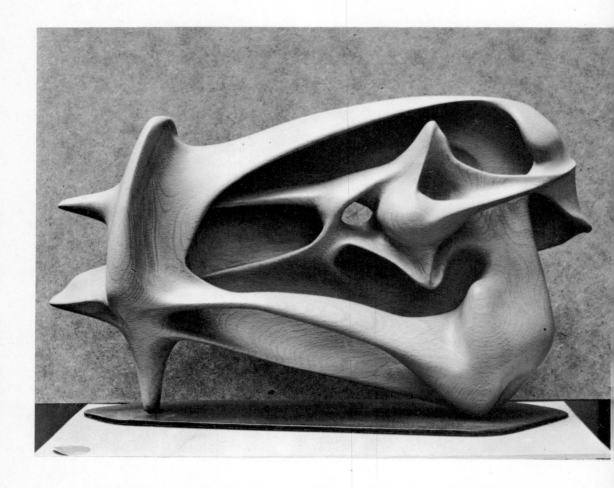

'Cion' (length 17 in., width 3 in., height 10½ in.) in beech—a wood sculpture deriving from a study of natural forms. Exhibited at the Royal Academy of Arts Summer Exhibition, 1961.

LEON UNDERWOOD (born 1890)

Leon Underwood studied at: Regent
Street Polytechnic 1907–10; Royal
College of Art 1910–13; Slade
School 1919–20.

'Totem to the Artist' (height 54 in. by
12 in. sq.), in English yew, made in 1963.
Exhibited at the Royal Academy
Summer Exhibition, 1964 and bought
by the Chantrey Bequest in 1964.
(Reproduced by courtesy of the
Trustees of the Tate Gallery, London)

Crèche figures (height 12 in.), in teak, made in 1960.

Crucifix (height 20 in.), in amyris, made in 1951 by Ferelyth Wills.

'Young donkey' (height 9 in.),
in mahogany.

'Hoopooe' (length 13 in.),
in mahogany.

D. G. LIGHT

'Patriarch', a relief (height 23 in.),
in oak, made in 1964.

J. de ALBERDI

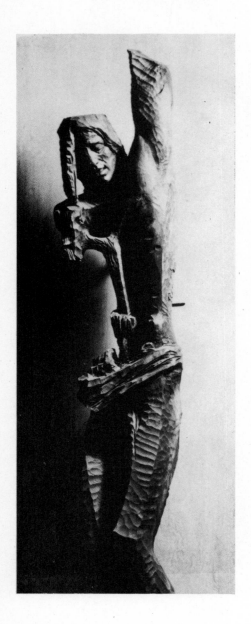

'He was Despised and Rejected'
(height 114 in.), in polychromed
walnut, made in 1955. Exhibited at
the Royal Academy of Arts
Summer Exhibition, 1964.

B. A. OXLEY (born 1910)

B. A. Oxley has been wood-turning almost as long as he can remember. He attended Sheffield College of Art, and had further training at Slough before starting up in business in 1933. He has been at Windsor since 1937.

Condiment set in elm, with sycamore spoons, 1950.
Heights: Pepper 2⅝ in.; Salt 1¼ in.; Mustard 2 in.—all made from 2⅛ in. square elm.

Turned dish (diameter 10½ in., thickness 1¼ in.) in English
walnut with marquetry monogram in thuya burr, sycamore
and ebony, made in 1957. The finished surface of the
dish is heat-proof.

JOHN BRIGGS

Bowl in English oak, turned on the lathe (diameter: outside
13 in., inside 3½ in.; height 1⅜ in.), made in 1956.

A. K. CLAIDEN (born 1919)

This designer has had a varied career which has included industrial work, social work and classes in schools for maladjusted children.

Hand-sculptured sugar bowls and spoons of natural plum, salt-cellars, and a long bowl of natural yew, all made in 1954. Each piece is worked individually and is unique. Each salt-cellar has a lip for pouring; the small salt-cellars are approximately $3\frac{1}{2}$ in. long.

Salad bowl (length 12 in. maximum width 7 in.) in yew, natural finish, made in 1955.

Hand-brush and hand-mirror in American black walnut, with
holly inlay, and a bowl in sapele, with holly inlay, designed
by G. Nixon Aldersley in 1958.

JAMES DAVIES (born 1876)

JAMES DAVIES is carrying on his family's generations-old tradition in the craft of wood-turning.

Turned wooden bowls made chiefly of sycamore, yew,
mahogany and plum, designed and made in 1950. The
bowls are usually 6 to 12 in. in diameter and 3 to 4 in. deep.

A. PETERS

Having served an apprenticeship with Edward Barnsley, A. Peters studied for two years at Shoreditch Training College and for six months at the L.C.C. Central School of Arts and Crafts. He is now teaching handicrafts. He has exhibited at The Crafts Centre of Great Britain since 1960.

Salad Bowl (10 in. dia., 3 in. deep) in Acacia, made in 1960.

Fruit bowl (12 in. dia., 3½ in. deep) in mahogany, made in 1958.

G. C. Dewey commenced his apprenticeship with a firm of wood-turners in 1916; he now has his own workshop.

Fruit bowl (10 in. dia., 3 in. deep) in oak; nut bowl (9 in. dia., 1½ in. deep) in brown oak; box with lid (3¼ in. dia., 3 in. high) in mahogany.

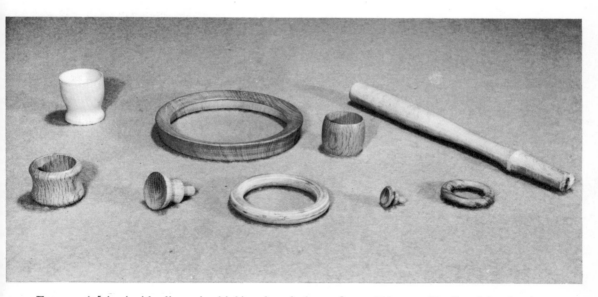

Egg cup (1⅝ in. inside dia., 2 in. high); rebated plaque frame (6 in. outside dia., ¾ in. deep); elliptical section hammer shaft 11½ in. long; serviette rings (1½ in. internal dia., 1⅜ in. high); ply ring (3¾ in. dia., ½ in. thick); small ring (2 in. dia., ⅜ in. thick); cupboard pulls (1½ in. dia. and ¾ in. dia.).

DARRELL WHITTAKER

Beaker (height 5⅜ in.), in mahogany.

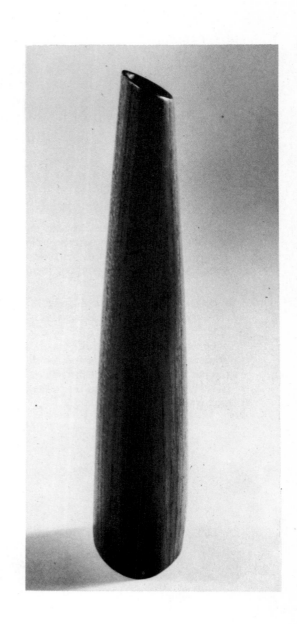

Ornamental vase (height 8⅝ in.), in
Burma teak, made by Darrell Whittaker.

Carved and engine-fluted wooden bowls and dishes (diameters 9 in. and 12 in., depths 3 in.) of sycamore, lime, cherry, walnut and yew, designed and made by DAVID W. PYE in 1950. The bowls and dishes have a variety of shapes which cannot be achieved by turning. The fluting-engine is a hand-driven and hand-guided machine.

Bowl in mulberry (approximately 18 in. diameter), designed and made by GUY NGAN at the School of Furniture Design, Royal College of Art, for the Harvard College Library Theatre Collection, 1955. As the mulberry timber was small and full of defects it was possible only to make up the small pieces of sound timber into a flat board, from which the bowl was made by cutting the flat sheet into a spiral pattern with a fretsaw. The bottom of the flat spiral was then pushed down to the required depth (determined by the pitch of the fretsaw cut), glue run into the joints, and the bowl turned in the ordinary way when the glue was set.

Prince Charles's bed. A christening present, made in yew, designed by FRANK GUILLE
and made in the School of Furniture Design, Royal College of Art, in 1950.
Motifs: silver and champlevé enamel enrichments designed and made by PHILIP POPHAM
of the School of Silversmithing and Jewellery, Royal College of Art.
Coverlet: designed by FRANK HOSWELL, School of Textile Design, Royal College of Art.
With acknowledgments to Her Majesty, Queen Elizabeth II.

J. H. EASDEN (born 1901)

J. H. Easden was trained in industry and at High Wycombe Technical College. Among his most notable works are the case for the gold salvers presented to H.M. the Queen on the occasion of the launching of the *Southern Cross*; the case for the mace, presented by the House of Commons to the Government of Rhodesia and Nyasaland; and tables and chair for the Worshipful Company of Carpenters' reinstated Court Room in the City of London.

J. H. Easden making the casket for the traditional glove used by Queen Elizabeth II at her Coronation in 1953. Made of oak from the timbers of Nelson's flagship *Victory*, the casket was lined with the same purple velvet from which the Coronation robe was made.

CRAFT ASSOCIATIONS

As a number of people mentioned in this book are members of The Crafts Council of Great Britain, the author is happy to include the following notes:

The Crafts Council of Great Britain was inaugurated in May 1964, and has come into being not only to draw attention to the existence of the crafts today, but to their growing importance in this age of automation and increasing leisure. The Council has many aims, the chief of them being to raise the level of craftsmanship in this country as well as the prestige of craftsmen.

The Council will provide more and more opportunities for craftsmen's work to be seen and commissioned, and it will give practical assistance to crafts organizations throughout the country.

The Crafts Council serves as a focal point not only for craftsmen and laymen in this country, but for crafts organizations throughout the world in co-operation with the World Crafts Council to which it is affiliated.

A permanent exhibition of the crafts, including furniture, is on view, at The Crafts Centre, 16 Hay Hill, Berkeley Square, London W.1.

INDEX

INDIVIDUALS

COLLEGES